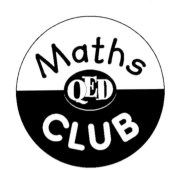

Maths
QED
CLUB

Multiplying

Ann Montague-Smith

QED Publishing

First published in the UK in 2005 by
QED Publishing
A Quarto Group company
226 City Road
London EC1V 2TT

www.qed-publishing.co.uk

A Catalogue record for this book is available from the British Library.

ISBN 1 84538 194 7

Written by Ann Montague-Smith
Designed and edited by The Complete Works
Illustrated by Peter Lawson
Photography by Steve Lumb

Publisher Steve Evans
Creative Director Louise Morley
Editorial Manager Jean Coppendale

Printed and bound in China

With thanks to:

Contents

Odds and evens

Play this game with a friend. You will each need a counter.
Take turns to toss a third counter onto the spinner below.
Move your counter to the first odd or even number.
Now it's your friend's turn. Keep doing this, moving to the
next odd or even number each time. The first one to 30 wins.

Start

0 1 2 3 4 5 6 7 8 9 10 11 12 13 14 15

Take turns to point to a number on the track.
Say if it is odd or even.

4

20 **21**
19 **22**
18 **23**
17 **24**
6 **25**

26 **27** **28** **29**
30
Finish

Even
Odd
Odd
Even
nner

Now try this
Play the game again.
This time take turns to roll
a 1–6 dice. Move your counter
the number of spaces you throw.
Tell your friend whether the number
you land on is odd or even.

5

2s, 3s, 4s, 5s and 10s

You will need red and blue counters. Count along the flowerpots in 2s. Put a red counter on each number you land on. Now count along in 4s and use blue counters. Which numbers have both blue and red counters? What can you say about these numbers?

Start
0 ➡ 1 ➡ 2 ➡ 3 ➡ 4

21 ⬅ 20 ⬅ 19 ⬅ 18 ⬅ 1⁊
⬇
22 ➡ 23 ➡ 24 ➡ 25 ➡ 26

Do this again for counting in 2s and 3s.

Challenge

Which is the first number that comes when you count in 2s and 3s? Yes, it's 6. Now which is the first number that comes when you count in 2s, 3s, 4s and 5s? You may find it helpful to use a number line.

0 1 2 3 4

5 → 6 → 7 → 8 → 9 → 10

6 ← 15 ← 14 ← 13 ← 12 ← 11

27 → 28 → 29 → 30 → 31

Finish

Using arrays

The bees have arranged the cells for their honey in arrays. Look at the array with 8 squares. It is 4 multiplied by 2, or 4x2. It can also be seen as 2x4. Look at the other arrays. Write a multiplication for each array.

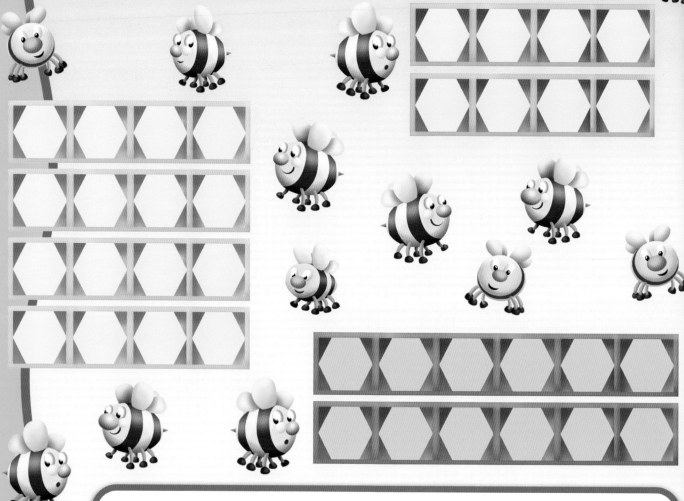

Can you write another multiplication for each array? Write how many cells there are in each array.

9

Doubling

You will need some counters. Choose a number on the sunken boat. Double it. Can you now find the doubled number? If so, cover both numbers with your counters. If you can't find the double, don't cover any number.

1	26	24	8
12	10	11	30
3	7	28	5

Can you find a way to cover all the numbers on the grid?

10

Find out

Investigate doubling numbers from 16 to 30. Write down the doubles of these numbers. Tell a friend how you worked out these doubles.

Double 16 is 32.

Double 17 is 34.

4 13 22 2

15 16 6 14

18 20 9

11

Multiplying by 2s and 10s

Read the multiplication on the card that the boy with blond hair is holding. Find the answer on a card that a girl is holding.

Now match the other multiplications to their answers. Which multiplication sentences have an odd answer?

8x2

10

4x10

40

16

Now try this

Think about all the answers to the questions from the 2 times-table. Is the answer each time odd or even? Is the answer each time in the 10 times-table odd or even? Can you think of a reason for your answers here?

6x2=12
3x10=30

100

70

6

7x2

9x2

13

Multiplication for 5s

The bees below are in groups of 5. How many groups are there? So how many bees are there altogether? Now look at the butterflies. They are also in groups of 5. Count the groups. How many butterflies are there altogether

Try this for the other groups of insects.

Draw your own groups of insects to show 9x5 and 10x5. Write how many in total there are each time.

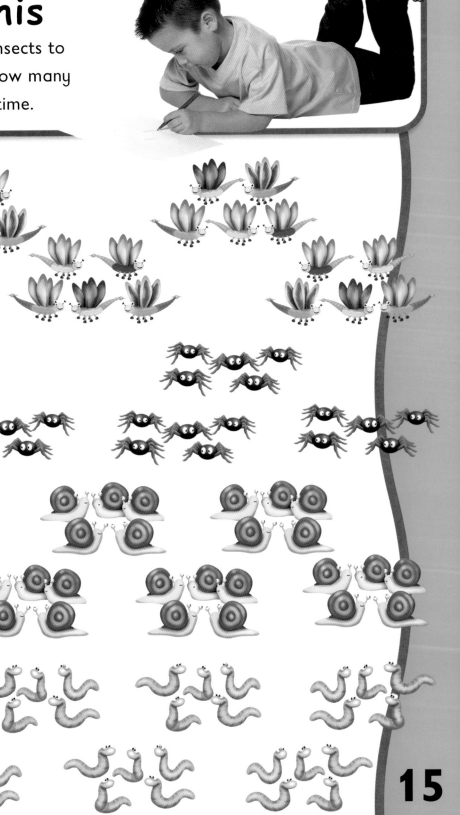

More doubles

The wind has blown away the answers to the double questions the animals are holding. Help the animals to find the answers

Which of these doubles are also a multiple of 10?
How can you tell?

80

30

25x2

20x2

100

50

45x2

35x2

Try this

Take turns to write down a number which is in the count of 5s, such as 5, 10, 15. Ask your friend to say its double. See how quickly you can do ten of these.

Double 15 is 30.

15

17

Number sort

Read the labels on the bags and decide where each number on the right should go. Some numbers can go into more than one bag.

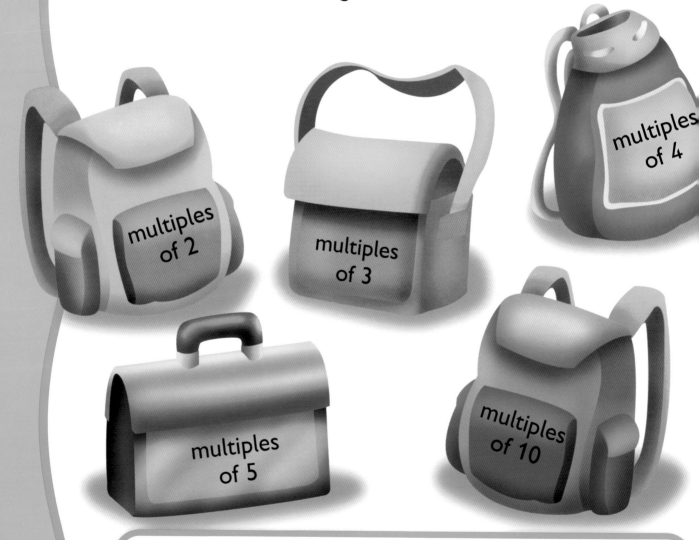

One of the numbers will not fit into any of the bags.
Can you find it?

6

32

27

12

Challenge

There was one number that would not fit into any of the bags. Think of some more numbers that will not fit. Can you find ten more of them?

11

40

2

30

16

60

45

7

25

9

15

19

How many vehicles?

Look at all the car and bicycle wheels below.
How many cars do the wheels belong to?
How many bicycles do the wheels belong to?

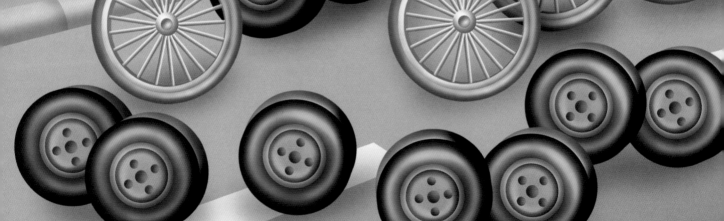

Talk about how you worked out the answer.

Challenge

Look again at the picture. Some cars have only three wheels. How many three-wheeled cars could there be?

21

Supporting notes

Odds and evens – pages 4–5

Count in 2s, from 0 to about 30, and say that these are the even numbers. Repeat this, but start on 1, and explain that these are the odd numbers. Children can count, jumping with their fingers along the pathway, to point to the odd or even numbers.

2s, 3s, 4s, 5s and 10s – pages 6–7

If children count correctly along the flowerpots, they will discover that certain numbers appear in counts of 2s and 4s, for example, 4, 8 and 12. They will also begin to see that the numbers that come in counts of 2s and 5s, are the decade numbers, as well as the numbers that come in counts of 10s. Similarly, by comparing counts of 2s and 3s, they will find the multiples of 6: 6, 12, 18… The *Challenge* answer is 60.

Using arrays – pages 8–9

An array is a rectangle which shows multiplication. Each array can be read in two ways, for example, 3x4 and 4x3. If children are unsure about this, help them to make their own rectangular arrays and ask them to count along one side, then along the adjoining side, so that they find the multiplication numbers. They can count all the cells to find the multiplication, for example, 4x3=12.

Doubling – pages 10–11

If children are unsure about the doubles of numbers to 15, then use some counters. Count out, say, 12, then another 12, match them to show that there are 2 sets of 12. Now ask the children to count on from 12: 13, 14, 15… 24 and agree that double 12 is 24.

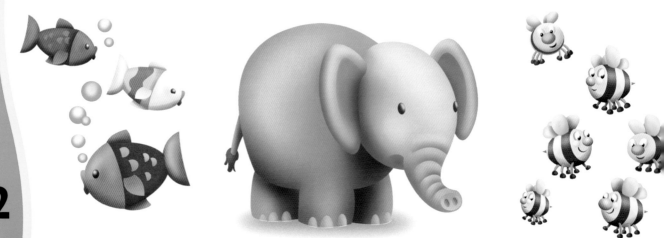

Multiplying by 2s and 10s – pages 12–13

Children need to have rapid recall of the multiplication facts for the 2 and 10 times-tables. If they are unsure about an answer, try counting in 2s or 10s, keeping a tally with fingers of how many 2s or 10s have been counted, until the required point in the count has been reached. For example, for 4x2 count 2, 4, 6, 8. So 4x2 is 8.

Multiplication for 5s – pages 14–15

Discourage children from counting each insect one by one. The activity is designed so that they should count in 5s: 5, 10, 15, 20… If the children are unsure about this, then count together in 5s. You may want to practise the count before starting the activity on the page.

More doubles – pages 16–17

This extends children's understanding of doubles to doubles of numbers in the 5 times-table. If children are unsure, count up from 0 in 5s to reach the start number. Ask, 'How many fives that? Now count on for the same number of 5s.' For example, to find double 20: 5, 10, 15, 20. That is 4 lots of 5. So 25, 30, 35, 40 gives another 4 lots of 5 to reach 40, or double 20.

Number sort – pages 18–19

If the children need more help with this activity, use the *2s, 3s, 4s, 5s and 10s* activity on pages 6 and 7. Now ask for each number on this page, 'Is it a multiple of 2? How can you tell? Is it a multiple of 3… 4… ?' Children may find it helpful to count in 2s, 3s, 4s… to check. The odd one out is 7, which is a prime number. Some numbers, such as 16 and 32 (multiples of 2 and 4) and 6 (multiple of 2 and 3) could go into either of the bags.

How many vehicles? – pages 20–21

The children need to count all the car wheels, then all the bicycle wheels. Suggest that they jot down on paper their totals. In order to work out how many cars there are, they may find it helpful to count in 4s, and keep a tally on their fingers, until they reach the total of wheels for the cars. Similarly, for the bicycles, they can count in 2s.

Using this book

The illustrations in this book are bright, cheerful and colourful, and are designed to capture the children's interest. Sit somewhere comfortable together, as you look at the book. Children of this age will normally be able to read most of the instructional words. Help with the reading where necessary, so that all children can take part in the activities, regardless of how fluent they are at reading at this point in time.

The activities cover the early concepts associated with multiplication. Children are encouraged to identify odd and even numbers and to count in 2s, 3s, 4s, 5s and 10s. They learn about arrays and how these can be read in two ways, for example, an array of 20 blocks in rows of 4s could be seen as 5x4 and 4x5. Children will also extend their knowledge of doubles.

If children are unsure about multiples of given numbers, encourage them to count in that number. So, for example, for multiples of 4, for 40, they can count four tens. Encourage them to keep a tally with their fingers to find the multiple. They will begin to realize, as with the arrays, that if they know 4x10=40 then 10x4=40. Over time, children should have rapid recall of the multiplication facts for 2s, 5s and 10s, and then for 3s and 4s. Learning to recite their tables 'parrot-fashion' has its place, but the practical activities in this book also help children to understand the processes involved in multiplication, so that the facts and how they are derived make sense.

Encourage the children to explain how they worked out the answers to the questions. Being able to explain their thinking, and to use multiplication vocabulary, helps the children to clarify in their minds what they have just done. Also, where there are children who are not so sure of how to solve the problem, hearing what others did, and how they did this, helps them to use these methods more effectively.

Do encourage children to make notes as they work at an activity. They can record numbers, writing them in order, or write simple sentences to explain. Encourage them to be systematic in the way that they work, so that they do not miss a vital part of the evidence that they need to find a solution.

Above all, enjoy together the mathematical games, activities and challenges in this book.